CONSERVATION OF WATER

CONSERVATION OF WATER

DR TAMANA BAHLOL

Contents

Acknowledgements v

1. Chapter 1 1

Acknowledgements

- Life without water is not possible. We need it for many things including cleaning, cooking, using the washroom, and more. Moreover, we need clean water to lead a healthy life.
- All in all, we must identify water scarcity as a real issue as it is very dangerous. Further, after identifying it, we must make sure to take steps to conserve it. There are many things that we can do on a national level as well as an individual level. So, we must come together now and conserve water.
- Water has become scarce due to a lot of reasons most of which are human-made. We exploit water on a daily basis. Industries keep discharging their waste directly into water bodies. Further, sewage keeps polluting the water as well.

1

- Introduction

  As we all know, water gives life to life and other creatures on earth. It is very important to continue life on Earth. Without water, life on any planet can not be imagined. Earth is the only planet in the entire universe, where water and life are in existence today. Therefore, we should not ignore the importance of water in our life and should try our best to save water by using all possible methods. Earth is surrounded by approximately 71% water, however, there is very little water to drink, the natural cycle of water balance automatically runs like rain and vaporization, however, the problem on earth is to protect the water and it is potable, which is very Available in small quantities. Water conservation is possible through good practice of people.

- Life without water is not possible. We need it for many things including cleaning, cooking, using the washroom, and more. Moreover, we need clean water to lead a healthy life.

- We can take many steps to conserve water on a national level as well as an individual level. Firstly, our governments must implement efficient strategies to conserve water. The scientific community must work on advanced agricultural reforms to save water.

Similarly, proper planning of cities and promotion of water conservation through advertisements must be done. On an individual level, we can start by opting for buckets instead of showers or tubs.

Also, we must not use too much electricity. We must start planting more trees and plants. Rainwater harvesting must be made compulsory so we can benefit from the rain as well.

Further, we can also save water by turning off the tap when we brush our teeth or wash our utensils. Use a washing machine when it is fully loaded. Do not waste the water when you wash vegetables or fruit, instead, use it to water plants.

All in all, we must identify water scarcity as a real issue as it is very dangerous. Further, after identifying it, we must make sure to take steps to conserve it. There are many things that we can do on a national level as well as an individual level. So, we must come together now and conserve water.

- Water has become scarce due to a lot of reasons most of which are human-made. We exploit water on a daily basis. Industries keep discharging their waste directly into water bodies. Further, sewage keeps polluting the water as well.
- The government must plan cities properly so our water bodies stay clean. Similarly, water conservation must be promoted through advertisements. On an individual level, we can start by fixing all our leaky taps. Further, we must avoid showers and use buckets instead to save more water.
- Water makes up 70% of the earth as well as the human body. There are millions of marine species present in

today's world that reside in water. Similarly, humankind also depends on water. All the major industries require water in some form or the other. However, this precious resource is depleting day by day. The majority of the reasons behind it are man-made only. Thus, the need for water conservation is more than ever now. Through this water conservation essay, you will realize how important it is to conserve water and how scarce it has become.

- Water Scarcity- A Dangerous Issue

Out of all the water available, only three per cent is freshwater. Therefore, it is essential to use this water wisely and carefully. However, we have been doing the opposite of this till now.

Every day, we keep exploiting water for a variety of purposes. In addition to that, we also keep polluting it day in and day out. The effluents from industries and sewage discharges are dispersed into our water bodies directly.

Moreover, there are little or no facilities left for storing rainwater. Thus, floods have become a common phenomenon. Similarly, there is careless use of fertile soil from riverbeds. It results in flooding as well.

Therefore, you see how humans play a big role in water scarcity. Living in concrete jungles have anyway diminished the green cover. On top of that, we keep on cutting down forests that are a great source of conserving water.

Nowadays, a lot of countries even lack access to clean water. Therefore, water scarcity is a real thing. We must deal with it right away to change the world for our future generations. Water conservation essay will teach you how.

- Water is the first need for anyone and water conservation is the hot topic today! It simply means making use of water in an appropriate and judicious manner. Since our lives depend entirely on water, it is our duty to think about water conservation and how we can contribute to it. To your knowledge, 97% of our planet is covered in salt water that we cannot use for drinking. The left side of 3% of the water is cool but the 2% is also blocked by glaciers and ice caps. So, we only have 1% left. So, now, feel something that explains why water conservation is important to us. We only depend on a small percentage of water, so it is our responsibility not to pollute and abuse it. Each of us must know how to save water.

- Water conservation methods

  A variety of methods can be used to keep water inside and out. Here they are:

  - By protecting the water against pollution, we can contribute to the conservation of water.

  - Water conservation can be done using water for redistribution.

  - Consider the rational use of groundwater.

- the use of recent or modern irrigation methods in the agricultural sector can also help save water.

  - By making changes in the culture model as if the crops are grown by farmers under agro-climatic conditions, there will be no need for excess water.

  - With the use of geothermal water.

  - Saving water in industries

  - With the help of management of the floods, water can also be saved.

  - Water can also be saved by guiding municipal agencies.

· Last but not least, water can also be conserved through the collection of rainwater. For example: digging lakes, canals, ponds to collect water, and then installing filtration systems to use it can be a great help. This water can easily be used for gardening, lawn irrigation or for toilets. You can also use stored water through rainwater harvesting for small-scale farming.

· Water is a priceless gift to humanity by nature. Life is possible only on earth because of water. People in India and other countries are struggling with water scarcity while three-fourths of the earth is surrounded by water. Due to the lack of water, people teach us to save and conserve water to protect the environment, life and world due to the difficulties faced by people in different areas.

Water is the most essential source of life on earth because we need water to perform all the tasks of life such as drinking, making food, bathing, clothing, and for harvesting etc. We need to save water for proper supply of water for future generation without polluting it. We must stop the waste of water, use water properly and maintain water quality.

Water is important for the survival of mankind. However, unfortunately, it is being ruined at a rapid pace around the world.

Water is a natural resource that is the cornerstone of all life forms, it is believed that the first form of life on Earth originated in water.

This clear liquid moves as the backbone of the living world, we have not only misused this resource but also made it scarce.

We have polluted the rivers, oceans and also disturbed the level of groundwater.

- Save Water Save Earth:

  We cannot imagine life on earth without water so we must realize that it is very important.

  According to research, it is known that only 1% of all freshwater on Earth. We, humans, are ruining it like anything, the day is not far when water will be as expensive as gold.

  There are several ways in which we are contributing to the waste of water given below:

  Leaving the tap open when not in use.

  Spraying water in lawns and parks when not needed.

  Not to reuse water:

  Most of the water can be reused so a lot of savings can be made.

  Polluting rivers and other water bodies.

  Unplanned Water Management.

  Deforestation also leads to loss of groundwater.

  We should also remember that about 70% of our body is water, how will we survive if there is not enough water on the earth.

  And we had wasted so much water in our daily activities such as washing cars, vegetables, clothes etc., soon a time will come when there will be little or no water for our existence.

- Water conservation is the only way to save water in the future to solve the problem of water scarcity

  the world, there is a major shortage of water, which has caused the common people to make long distances for drinking water and also to make necessary water to meet everyday tasks. On the other hand, in adequate water areas, people are wasting more water than their daily needs. We all need to understand the importance of water and problems related to lack of water in the future. We should not ruin and pollute useful water in our life and encourage water conservation and conservation amongst the people.

Water is a precious gift for our life on earth by God, according to the availability of water on earth, we can understand the importance of water in our lives. Everything on the earth and all life forms needs water, such as humans, animals, trees, insects and other animals. The balance of water on the earth is through some processes such as rainfall and evaporation. Three-fourths of the Earth's water is surrounded by water, whereas very few percent of water is available for human use. Therefore, there is a problem with the lack of clean water which can end life.

Clean water is a very important element of life, so to protect the future, we need water conservation. If we save water, then we save life on the whole world and on earth. Water is called universal liquid, hence it is the main ingredient in assuring quality of life. We should pledge to use it according to the need of water so that it can be polluted without mixing it together. Water pollution will save us by preventing other dirt and industrial pollution in water. Proper pollution management should be done, all of which must be followed.

- To maintain the existence of life on Earth, the protection and protection of water is very important because life without water is not feasible. As an exception in the entire universe, water helps in continuing the life cycle on earth because the earth is the only planet where water and life exist. Water is our life, so only we are responsible for saving it. According to the operation of the United Nations, it has been found that girls do not go to school in Rajasthan because they have to travel long distances to bring water, which laps all day, so they do not get time for any other work.

According to the survey of National Crime Records Bureau, it has been recorded that about 16,632 farmers (2,369 women) have lost their lives due to suicide, although 14.4% due to drought is the reason that we can say that India And in other developing countries there is also lack of water due to illiteracy, suicides, fighting and other social issues. In such areas of water scarcity, children of future generations can not get the right to live with their basic education and live happily.

Being a responsible citizen of India, we must be aware of all the problems of water scarcity so that we can fulfill all the promises and go ahead for water conservation. It is right to say that small efforts of all people can give a bigger result, such as drop-down, a pond, river and ocean can become us, we do not have to make extra efforts for water conservation, we have our daily There is a need to make some positive changes in the activities like after each use, after using the bucket for washing or bathing instead of faucet, fountain or pipe, and use mugs. A small effort of millions of people can give a big positive result towards the water conservation campaign.

By assessing very low percentage of safe and safe drinking water on the earth, water conservation or water conservation campaigns have become very important for all of us. Due to industrial wastes, large sources of water are being polluted daily to promote the proper water management system by promoters in all industrial buildings, apartments, schools, hospitals etc. to bring more efficiency in saving water. needed.

The common people should run an awareness program to learn about possible problems with drinking water or lack of water. There is an urgent need to eliminate the behavior of ordinary people about the wastage of ordinary water.

People at the village level should collect water for rain water. Rainwater can be saved by small or large ponds with proper maintenance. Young students need more awareness and should concentrate on solutions and problems of this problem. Living in many countries of developing countries is affecting insecurity and lack of water. More than 40 percent of the global population live in supply demand areas. And in the coming decades, this situation can get worse as everything will grow like populations, agriculture, industry etc.

- Why should we save water?

To answer the water to save us, first you need to know the importance of water, that is why water is valuable in our lives. Without oxygen, water and food life is not possible. Lokin is the most important water in all three. Now the question arises that the percentage of pure water is present on earth.

According to statistics, it is estimated that less than 1% of the water on the earth is potable. If we get the full ratio of drinking water and population of the world, then more than one billion people live in the world 1 gallon of water every day. It has also been assessed that by 2025 more than 3 billion people will be facing water scarcity.

Now people have started to understand the importance of clean water, although they are not trying to save water completely. There is a good habit to save water, and everyone should do their best to keep life on earth. Some years ago, no one used to sell water in the shop, although now the time has changed so much and now we can see that the pure water bottle is being sold everywhere. In the past, the first people were surprised to see the water sold in the shops, however, now, they are ready to give 20 rupees per bottle or more for their good health. We can clearly understand that there will be a shortage of clean water all over the world in the coming years. Below, we have given some facts that will tell you that clean water has become so valuable to us today:

Many people die due to waterborne diseases, more than 4 million.

Most developing countries suffer from clean water deficiency and diseases caused by dirty water.

About 300 liters of water is spent in preparing a one-day newspaper, so distribution of news channels should be encouraged.

Due to diseases caused by water, one child dies every 15 seconds.

People around the world have started using water bottles, which cost $ 60 to $ 80 billion per year.

In rural areas of India, Africa and Asia, people have to decide for a long distance (about 4 km to 5 km) for clean water.

People are suffering due to water borne diseases in India, due to which India's economy is very much affected.

- Ways to save water

We shared some great ways to save water without making any changes in our lifestyle. Domestic members spend 240 liters of water per day for household tasks. A small family with a four-member family spends 960 liters per day and 350400 liters per year. Only 3% of the total consumption of water is used for drinking and cooking of food, the rest of the water is used for other plants such as drinking water, bathing etc. laundry etc.

Some general prescriptions for water conservation:

Everyone should understand their own responsibility and avoid using excess water as well as cooking water and food.

If gradually all of us will start saving water to the Garden, by pouring water into the toilet, cleaning it etc., saving per excess water will be possible.

We should save the rain water for defecation, laundry, and water for the purpose of drinking water.

We must collect rain water and drink it for cooking.

We should wash our clothes only in the washing machine when it is clothed to our full potential. In this way, we will save 4500 liters of water as well as electricity per month.

Use buckets and mugs instead of showering with shower, which will save 150 to 200 liters of water per year.

We should stop our tap properly after every use, which will save 200 liters of water every month.

Due to the excessive use of water during Holi festival, it should be encouraged to dry and safe.

To save ourselves from the water wastage, we must be aware of the news of the people who are struggling daily for each drop of water for their living.

To spread awareness, we should promote programs related to water conservation.

Do not allow more water in the cooler to be wasted during the summer season, only use the required amount.

We should not destroy the pipe by putting water on the lawn, house or roads.

Promote planting in the rainy season so that the plants get natural water.

We should make a habit of washing our hands, fruits, vegetables etc with water utensil instead of the open tap.

We should refrain from giving water to plants till 11 o'clock in the afternoon as they evaporate at that time. By giving water in the morning or evening, the plants absorb water well.

We should promote planting which is dry tolerable.

We should encourage family members, children, friends, neighbors and co-workers to adopt or adopt this process by the end to get positive results.

- One of the items people, animals, and our environment cannot live without is water. Water is extremely vital in the everyday life of everyone in the world from everyday life of drinking, washing clothes, animals, grains, cleaning, and so many other uses that eliminating water would eliminate our species as we all depend on the necessity of water. "The water footprint refers to the volumes of water consumption and pollution that are 'behind' your daily consumption".

The global consequences of using so much water are that globally we are in awater crisis. The demand for water is always a necessity and as population increases the need for water increases. The lack of safe drinking water and sanitation varies from country to country. "More than one out of six people lack access to safe drinking water, namely 1.1 billion people, and more than two out of six people lack adequate sanitation, namely 2.6 billion people. 2900 children die every day from water borne diseases".

- The global consequences of using so much water are that globally we are in awater crisis. The demand for water is always a necessity and as population increases the need for water increases. The lack of safe drinking water and sanitation varies from country to country. "More than one out of six people lack access to safe drinking water, namely 1.1 billion people, and more than two out of six people lack adequate sanitation, namely 2.6 billion people. 2900 children die every day from water borne diseases".

- Water is essential for life on earth. Water is needed for growing food, keeping ourselves clean, generating power, controlling fire and most importantly to stay alive! This list is simply non-ending. This shows that water is an integral part of our daily life and we are heavily dependent on it. the usage of water and recycling of waste water for different purposes such as cleaning, manufacturing, and agricultural irrigation.

- Conserving water saves you money! Not only will your water bill go down, but as you use less water, your gas or energy bill will also decline. If your whole community conserves, you will also pay less fees for water-related services. Water conserving communities will not need to pay as much to develop new supplies and expand or upgrade water and wastewater infrastructure.
Wise usage of water helps us in saving money.